PATHWAY TO PROSPERITY

PATHWAY TO PROSPERITY

MARLOWE SINCLAIR

CONTENTS

CHAPTER 1

Introduction

This personal financial plan offers a roadmap to attain financial freedom. This is the final milestone of your financial journey, where you have accumulated enough wealth to sustain yourself and your dependents for your lifetime, without your regular work income. Financial freedom covers retirement, or in case you are working but doing it out of a personal choice and not out of necessity, or in a situation where there is a change in career or personal choice to pursue something different. Financial freedom is about the freedom to choose your lifestyle, work or anything you want to do because you are accumulating enough money to choose to do something you enjoy rather than something that is mandatory. You have the flexibility to invest time in yourself, your family, travel or philanthropy without any constraints. In any form, financial freedom means financial stress and worry is permanently and comfortably resolved.

Whether you have just started earning income or currently are not investing and need to start, or you have been investing your annual savings for some time but getting lost in the numerous products and can't find a direction, or you are already investing and seeking more sophisticated asset allocation strategies, it does not matter because the roadmap presented in this book would help you all. At the end of the roadmap, there are different routes to attain financial freedom which have been uniquely calibrated based on your risk profile and the various decision points relevant to your stage in life. All customized roadmaps share both a specific endpoint goal (the desired financial freedom value at the end of the period) and a specific investment strategy (where you put in your savings). The investment strategy suggested in the roadmap is to start with simple and safe savings products that gradually transition towards more investment strategy products. In the end, the only goal should be to reach the milestone of financial freedom for yourself while simultaneously providing clarity on other lifecycle events.

CHAPTER 2

Understanding Financial Freedom

Understanding the concept helps you avoid setting disproportionate amounts of energy, time, and resources in an activity that in and of itself cannot fulfill your deeper aspirations. Spend too little time and money on seeking financial freedom, however, and you may never reach the status of freedom you desire. Understanding the science behind meeting that status is just as important. It can be a motivator to reprogram your spending habits, to increase your savings, and to invest in tools that will minimize the hazards that may otherwise prevent you from achieving it.

Financial freedom is the ability to live the lifestyle you desire without having to work or rely on anyone else for money. This is achieved after all of your essential living expenses (housing, transportation, food, insurance, taxes, clothing, etc.) are met by income sources not directly tied to your own time. Instead of pursuing this as an end in itself, it's helpful to understand the unseen forces that are driving you to seek it: autonomy, self-actualization, time, legacy, and spiritual growth.

CHAPTER 3

Assessing Your Current Financial Situation

For assessing your current financial situation, we suggest starting with your current balance. As of today, what are your assets? We suggest having a positive net worth. Let's continue by evaluating your current monthly income. What are your sources of income? How much time do you work for each income? Are you happy with this income? Is it enough for your current needs? After evaluating your current level of income, we suggest registering your monthly expenses. It is very important to detail all the expenses. Finally, do you have a surplus or deficit every month? Based on your current situation, are you able to save? A good assessment of the level of savings relative to your current level of income allows us to locate and make the necessary adjustments. What can you do to increase your income and reduce your current expenses? In your current level of expenses, are the monthly payments necessary for extraordinary purchases?

Welcome to this module on assessing your financial situation. In the next 20 minutes and in this presentation, we will explain step by step how to evaluate your current financial situation. In every financial journey, you have to start where you are. And the first question has to be, how deep in trouble are you? And when we talk about financial troubles, only financial troubles, we are talking good. We will guide you on how to do a full-fledged diagnosis of your current financial situation, and later on, you can take the steps necessary to correct course.

CHAPTER 4

Setting Financial Goals

To achieve long-term financial goals, work on them in smaller sections to help monitor progress and avoid feeling overwhelmed. As they are expected to take longer periods, usually more than a year to accomplish, it can be challenging to stay on track and committed. When setting long-term goals, take the time to list your priorities and develop a plan of action to keep you focused and motivated. Think about a mixture of goals, such as traveling or purchasing a home. Those goals will allow you to indulge in rewarding experiences, which will further motivate and keep you aimed at the financial plan. Include friends or family members in your financial journey to share your successes and offer encouragement.

Financial short-term goals are those where you expect the outcome to happen soon, most likely in a year's time. As short-term goals are very close to being achieved, they should be easier to work on. An example of a short-term financial goal may be saving $500 for a two-week holiday in 45 weeks. Also, consider adding another goal of paying off a particular bill, in addition to saving for the holiday.

A financial goal is a target to strive for to guide and motivate you as you work towards a budget, saving money, and investing. When developing financial goals, it is important to be specific so that you will be able to see the progress of your financial journey. For example, saying "I want to be financially free" is not specific enough, whereas stating, "I would like to reach a million dollars before the age of 30" is more descriptive. While a specific goal can motivate you to achieve, one that is not precise may cause you to lose focus. Try to set at least one or two short-term goals and two to three long-term goals.

CHAPTER 5

Creating a Budget

We certainly could spend hours on what I call a real accounting, based on a detailed budget, to help us make better decisions, but time does not permit this. Therefore, I'm going to focus specifically on the concept of the budget for now.

After we folded our business, we went into debt for one whole year and possibly more. In just one single year or less, I see why our business did not succeed. It was because there was no solid plan (without seeing the numbers). After the year is out, our decreasing money situation confirms what the numbers had indicated for quite some time.

During my first attempt at making a budget, it became obvious to me immediately that I could work that many years for that same pay and I would be in no better position than I was right then. It also became obvious to me, with one look at the numbers, why our small family business had to fold. I wanted my hard work to mean something.

I was crestfallen. I loved my job, but I was struggling just to put food on our table. So I did the first thing that came to mind: I prepared a budget. I had never put together a real budget; I thought I knew where my money was coming from and where it was going.

A few years later, a friend of mine, who worked at the same company but for a different owner, let it slip that he made nearly twice as much as I did doing essentially the same thing. He was honest about the numbers, and while they were not exact, they were close.

An example of how budgets work: Sometimes you may not realize how doing just a few things differently can make a huge difference in reaching your goals. I once worked for a non-profit corporation, which of course did not pay very well. I just saw what they were going to pay me, and I was happy that it was a full-time job and happy that I could stay home with my babies. Without seeing how they expected me to live off that little money, I thought it was a lot of money. It looked like a lot on paper, but when it came down to it, it was not much.

Creating a budget to establish financial goals is a good way to find money that you thought you didn't have. It may sound like a boring and time-consuming task, and can even be anxiety-inducing, but trust me, it's worth it.

CHAPTER 6

Saving and Investing

In an age where financial management and discipline are no longer options but needs, individuals need to possess the knowledge, skills, and perspective required to balance consumption and saving. In line with this objective, a reliable educational institution is your best ally in educating yourself the proper way of investing and saving your money correctly.

On the other hand, investing your money requires proper investment techniques and skillful selection of investments. It also demands that you monitor its performance. The reward for doing your homework beforehand and a bit of legwork on the monitoring would make it safer, correct, and sound. When the time shares or stocks are down or bad, it means that with your extra money, you can buy more of these at a low price, which eventually translates to more profits in the future when the share prices go up again.

The word "proper" refers not as much to legit or legal, but more to rationale or correctness. It also implies prioritization of saving money before spending it on important, but often unnecessary, things. Saving money serves as great insurance and standby funds for the future. It gives peace of mind, especially when you know that you have stashed your hard-earned money aside for future consumption.

CHAPTER 7

Managing Debt

If you are ready to attack your existing debt, there is something called the debt snowball plan. This is a debt reduction strategy and an enhancement to paying off the minimum to the most indebted accounts. It resulted in behavioral and financial benefits to the user as they incrementally paid off owed balances. To add to this, with each owed balance reduction, you can have a powerful psychological boost and lend a payoff to a new, more significant debt balance. Similar to investing or other financial goals, the initial funding rate and duration of entrance into trading costs should be only targeted minimally and lowly than other risky securities. By using this model, an individual is inclined towards success against the smaller, more quickly paid off balances, and away from increasing the chance of paying off more costly debt.

To get started, it's good to check in on what debts you currently have. This might mean making a list of all debts that are in your name or affect your credit. Hit the online accounts, sift through the mailed statements, and give the creditors a call if you cannot find a balance online. This might serve as concrete evidence and motivation to begin your journey to reduce your debts. Against each named debt, you should document and summarize the balance owed, the interest rate paid, the monthly minimum payment, and any other important features of the debt that may not be immediately apparent. This is an action step of your roadmap, and the one that will empower you to begin action items to start addressing your debts.

To effectively save and invest for your future, you need to avoid the shackles of debt. There are times where debt may be useful, however, it is best to be avoided if possible. It's always best to pay off debt before starting to save money. The longer you put off paying off the debts, the harder and more costly those debts are to pay off. It's more difficult to save for your important financial goals. You might have higher balances, incur interest and late fees, and harm your long-run credit and financial health.

CHAPTER 8

Building Multiple Streams of Income

Collecting passive income is a good reason to start a small business. A small business that generates small profits is a good way to make small additional possessions to create wealth. The equity you build in a small business is sold for a large payment later in life. That is why have an aim that you hope to achieve as an entrepreneur. Create and grow a small business as a way to create a lot of videos or a lot of articles. Meanwhile, create and profit from the energy of variable numerous sources. With every video or post, more potential income can be created due to the growth of a significant number of streams of income.

Apple's iPhone is an example of a company that has achieved this with continued innovation since its introduction in 2007. A company like Apple today has more money in the bank than some entire countries. Investing in their success can be a passive form of income as the company generates a profit. As a shareholder, you now own a small piece of the company, and as the value of Apple stock goes up, so does the value of your share.

Where do these multiple streams come from? Rich people have several types of income that come without their permanent presence at work. Their money makes money for them in multiple ways. They have money coming in from real estate, dividend stocks, money growing in a retirement account, royalties or licensing agreements, and revenues should be diversified as well as significant.

Multiple streams of income are a must for obtaining a stage in life where you can worry less about your financial situation and focus more on things that really matter. More than two-thirds of self-made millionaires have at least three streams of income. That comes to show that you can't depend on just one source of income. With just one source, you are just one sick day, one duffle and dumb CEO, less company, or one loss away from being in financial trouble. Multiple streams of income are the way to go.

CHAPTER 9

Protecting Your Wealth

In this guide, valuable time and effort have been put into discussing how to make a rich life rather than just a rich bank account. A rich bank account without freedom is not the goal of life. Unfortunately, during troubled times, such as war or economic depression, wealth is not only at risk in financial structures, but there might even be confiscations by repressive governments or additional taxes to burden wealthier people even further. It is important to do everything and anything to protect your wealth and assure your future in the best way possible. These are some of the things to take into account when protecting your wealth:

- Make sure to have all future payments of your future upfront. (Example: Rent from your properties, payable interests from companies, etc.) That way you do not have to make predictions about future income nor wait for those regular payments. People who are retired, for example, should already have their retirement income given to them once and for all. By doing so, you protect their income in terms of the economic highs and lows that exist. - Consider geographic diversification with different assets in different countries, thus avoiding the expropriation of government money and taking advantage of existing opportunities in certain economies. (Example: Investing in a forest owned in Australia, in a cottage in Argentina, in real estate in the south of the United States, with the government money being one in a Swiss bank, another in U.S. dollars, and the third in gold). - Pay attention to the formation of your portfolio. Having money in the stock market may not mean good diversification. In case of armed conflict, monetary deflation, or other catastrophes, the way of recovering financially would be by investing in stocks capable of surviving such situations. - In some cases, PPS should be avoided. Its success was very notable because it is important to have the majority of one's income produced by rent or interests. However, if the country adopts socialist measures in times of crisis, will the money stored in PPS not be expropriated one way or the other?

CHAPTER 10

Planning for Retirement

Start planning for your retirement as soon as possible. It means that from day one of your working life, you should start thinking of what your retirement will look like. You don't need to retire at the same age as the previous generation. With the right planning, it is possible to start planning for retirement. This will give you an indication of the approximate amount you will need to accumulate for a comfortable retirement. The rest of this article establishes targets and offers more information to help you with retirement planning.

Retirement: Nobody wants to think about retirement. After all, it's so far off and seems like a separate world. Some people are in denial and actually believe they'll never retire. Others, who understand the concept of retirement, feel they are invincible and can always earn enough money to retire in style. The truth is you already are working so that one day you can retire. Maybe you are accumulating savings without this being your intention, and your retirement years may be more than you can afford. Planning for your retirement is a huge endeavor, and the sooner you start, the less amount you'll have to put away in the future. You must feel motivated to start planning for retirement. Remember: nobody cares more about your well-being than you do.

CHAPTER 11

Estate Planning

In order to have a plan, you need to start with the basics. Question is - do you have a will? If you and your partner die without a will, it can create a huge mess for your family. In case you have minor children, you especially need to have a will in place. That way, you can appoint a guardian or guardians for your children who will fight and work to raise them. They would be provided for financially in case something were to happen. If you have a will, you can specify in your will who will raise your children. We have a trust so my parents don't have to deal with the legal system at the worst time of their life. What most people don't realize is that when the kids are minors, the vast majority of the estates are controlled by the legal system. In essence, the court may tell my parents how to spend on our kids. I wouldn't want to put my parents through that. I also wouldn't want to put my kids through the trauma of what money can do to a family and them personally.

I have an important message for you. If you don't do this now, your family could be left out in the cold if something were to happen to you. Question is - are you prepared for it? Trust me, life is unpredictable. We never know what could happen, when it could happen, where it could happen or how it could happen. This deep reality can wake someone up to the fact that it is extremely important to be prepared. Below, we have covered some essential documentation required in case something happens. We pray to the universe that these never have to be used.

CHAPTER 12

Tax Strategies

Passive, Portfolio, and Material Participant Business Activities - Generally, the passive or non-passive status of an investor in a particular business activity is based on the investor's direct involvement or lack thereof in the day-to-day operations of that activity, relative to a set number of hours of active participation threshold. A passive business activity is any business activity that involves the conduct of any trade or business, and in which the taxpayer does not materially participate. Other than for the determination of which activities count as "real estate professional" activities with regard to the 2013 3.8% net investment income tax established by the Patient Protection and Affordable Care Act and the 15.1% self-employment Hungarian Income Tax Withholding and Reporting Requirements created by Schedule SE, a material participant business activity is an activity that involves the conduct of any trade or business, in which the taxpayer will be considered a material participant as a result of their performance of services in any tax year if: (1) the taxpayer participates in the activity for more than 100 hours during the tax year, excluding those hours devoted to traveling to and from the business activity, and which are hours that do not involve performing services in connection with the operation of the business activity; and (2) the taxpayer's participation satisfies the facts and circumstances test that the taxpayer (i) participates in the activity for more than 500 additional hours during the tax year, excluding those hours devoted to traveling to and from the business activity, and which are hours that do not involve performing services in connection with the operation of the business activity; and (ii) meets this 500-hour participation test only if the taxpayer's involvement in the activity is substantially all of the participation by any individual engaged in the activity, including individuals who are not owners of the activity; and (3) in the case of a husband and wife joint tax return filing, wherein both spouses have made the election under 469(c)(7)(A) for the tax year (meeting the 500-hour test as such, and provided that each spouse separately satisfies the first material participation test of devoting more than 100 hours in the tax year to the business activity, excluding those hours devoted to traveling to and from the business activity, and which are hours that do not involve performing services in connection with the operation of the business activity), each of the spouses shall be treated as materially participating in the business activity if and only to the extent that the other spouse would have been treated as a materially participating individual in such activity if the other spouse itemized their time as material participation by the other spouse in the business activity on an attached election statement described in section 1.469-10(g)(3)(ii).

From a tax standpoint, the Internal Revenue Code organizes activities into three basic groups, making it easier to optimize tax benefits based on your business level decisions. That is, whether it is a passive, active, or portfolio business activity that you are involved in. The Internal Revenue Code considers you to be involved in either passive business activities, portfolio business activities, or material participant business activities.

CHAPTER 13

Building a Strong Credit Score

That last tip, setting up a small but revolving balance on your open accounts, may be more critical if you can't seem to qualify for installment loans. It will demonstrate that you can, every month, obtain a loan – albeit a small one – and are able to service it. Many of the other methods of improving a poor credit score, like keeping your old(er) accounts open or getting family members to add you to their cards, benefit those who already have good credit, which first-time borrowers won't have. Repeating this step can increase the number of results of the other methods listed in this article.

Use your cards regularly and pay in full, and set up a small, revolving balance.

There are no real shortcuts in this business, but building a good credit is more about being consistent over many years than about making the best short-term decisions. Take these steps often enough and if you can, start early, and the rest will tend to fall into place.

CHAPTER 14

Achieving Financial Independence

You start by increasing your yearly savings rate over time. You can start by setting an easy lower SR the first year and gradually adding 1% to your SR each and every year until you reach your desired SR for your TI. This increase will force you to live frugally by embracing simple living, giving you the chance to take advantage of the magic of compounding. For the first few years, all of your contributions may seem so small that it may seem as if almost nothing is occurring. Nevertheless, keep adding to your investment earnings. Adding over time will seem as if your investment earnings are adding more and more to themselves, just like your education. If you keep adding to your strengths in your field, over time, they all become accumulated, helping you get better at your job. Remember those previously tiny contributions to your investment earnings? The contributions, combined with all of the earnings on interest and gains, continue to grow. And as they grow, each year your investment gains get accumulated over the previous year's contributions, so that you may have been investing $19,500 at the end of the year and adding an extra $250 when your SRs become bigger. By the time you reach age 70, these increases will be even larger, since your contributions will keep earning more in interest and dividends.

Finally, you will focus on achieving financial independence. You start by setting your FI number, a long-term goal, by increasing your savings rate (SR), using tax-advantaged accounts, avoiding lifestyle creep by paying yourself first, taking advantage of the magic of compounding, and by setting and using a strategy.

CHAPTER 15

Overcoming Financial Challenges

Overcoming Financial Challenges: Financial peace is within our reach, especially when we have the exact steps we need to take. If your financial questions are about saving, budgeting, paying off debt, or investing, we are here to empower you. It's time to tackle your financial dreams! This is a week for empowerment and transformation. With the exact steps and tactical advice needed to start making real changes, any financial dream can become a reality. Does this even sound crazy? If you need help, follow these steps and let's start making progress!

The day we achieve financial peace will be one of the greatest days of our lives. On that beautiful day, the financial headaches of our past will fade into distant memory. Today, The Chris Hogan Show is focusing on the financial challenges we can all face and the exact steps we need to take to overcome them. We have some great callers on the line looking for help. Michelle talks to Chris about the financial challenges she and her husband are facing. Tim shares his dream of being part of the military. And then there's Jamie, who is ready to invest after tackling her debt. Let's get going!

CHAPTER 16

Embracing a Wealth Mindset

Remember to take inventory of your essential success components. Determine what you seek in each area, and then get on with the business of framing your personal financial security drawing in word, image, or other form. Access your path. Get started on your trek toward realizing your potential importance in the overall equation.

Each of us has an individual responsibility to ourselves and to our family members to embrace a wealthy mindset. The wealthy help others to become wealthy. This occurs when we become secure with our own wealth - or lack thereof. Again, this does not happen by chance. There is a combination of knowledge, perspective, personal responsibility, and patience that combine to lead us toward financial security. The wealthy understand that health, wealth, happiness, family freedom, and personal growth all affect one another. It is difficult to be happy when you are ill, just as enjoyment in family life is compromised if personal freedom is hampered. There simply is not one variable of these success components that takes precedence over another. They all relate to one another, and for this reason, all are equally important.

Where do we begin in crafting our picture of the desired outcome? It always starts with a question, "If you could have everything you wanted in life, what would that be?" Our responses always include financial security, health, happiness, personal growth, safety, freedom, and family.

When planning your blueprint, refer to Section 14, "Painting Your Wealth Picture." By drawing and painting the picture, you are solidifying your foundation of financial freedom. The more you can focus, envision, and clarify your financial destination, the more certain you are to arrive. It's one thing to have a vague notion of where you want to live and how you would like your children to travel, or how you want to help your parents live out their later years; it's something entirely different to be able to paint the picture vividly within your mind's eye. By doing so, potential obstacles that present themselves during your journey will be seen as simply temporary deviations in the road, suggesting which direction to take as adjustments for your destination.

CHAPTER 17

Developing Financial Discipline

That sounds good, but the person knows their future financial picture will continue to get brighter every day, and then they must inevitably deal with anxiety for immediate results. Adapting the philosophy, you must also never give up your financial goals. This fear of the unknown tends to delay people from developing their financial discipline when they are really young and most likely their wealth goals are far off in their future. Goals of increasing our financial discipline to ensure our long-term wealth are simple to state. It is never expanding our budget to the newfound resources when our assets create new wealth from interest, dividends, and growth. Because of the cognitive dissonance with feeling satiated from the resources that were hard to build our current position, you must only focus on how it will cause you to attain your financial goals.

Developing a financial discipline to create the wealth you desire can be summed up in a simple phrase: "Never give up your goals." People spend about 3 hours a week to more than 2 hours a day daydreaming or just plain wasting time. Beginning with a penny, each subsequent payment is doubled. Would you rather have a million dollars now or a penny doubled every day for 30 days? Besides developing discipline, this simple math problem gives a practical understanding of the power of compounding money.

CHAPTER 18

Cultivating Money-Saving Habits

Once you've taken our specific suggestions, consider ways to hone your efforts even further by acting on any remaining flabby spending that wasn't addressed by our recommended list. If you're having trouble finding areas of waste, you might need to take a fresh look at your entire financial life. Every cent counts. Not because being a miser is such a smart financial strategy, but because by correcting these areas, you're controlling how you spend the only thing you can't control - where money goes. Most of us don't come naturally with money-saving habits. Unfortunately, although our habits were well-intentioned, we often added expenses without regard for where they ultimately lead in terms of our financial empowerment. The lesson here is that by systematically incorporating specific actions in your life on a regular basis, no matter how committed you are to your original budgeting practices, it's easy to spend more than you anticipated if you lack solid controls around your spending behaviors. Shifting from the habit of saving and only thinking about wealth creation to directly creating your prosperity through direct action is the intent behind our roadmap.

So much of what we do is habit. 40% of the decisions we make every day are habits. With money, all our hundreds of decisions result in thousands of impacts. By cultivating good habits, you can create a wealth-producing financial strategy that will continue long after its implementation. Saving money is a foundational element of accumulating savings. The foundation of being able to gain wealth is to avoid spending more than necessary. You can always earn more money, but you can never earn more time; wasted money through inefficient spending always leads to wasted time. The life-blood of financial freedom is both the ability to manage and to effectively save money. Fortunately, we've outlined challenges with expense management and provided suggestions for increasing your money-saving awareness in Chapter 1.

CHAPTER 19

Investing in Real Estate

In general, when people look into investing, the typical things that come to mind are stocks. This is by far the most publicized method of investing, but there are in fact many other methods. So, are stocks a good way to invest? For short-term speculation (under 5 years), the methods that can be detailed to increase returns for investment in real estate would not be worth the time invested. I would suggest searching for a successful day trader (short-term stock market speculator). Long-term investing in stocks, however, does offer good returns if sustained through many years (7 – 10). Diversification, good stocks to purchase, excellent rates of return (30%), all are common suggestions. Bus tours, education seminars, and mutual funds in general are non-profit yet for investment vehicle shops. A lot of people will agree that it may take 90% of the returns from the investor. With real estate investing, the typical investment vehicle shops may charge 10%.

In general, the only way average people have the ability to create extraordinary wealth is through real estate investing. Most other investment vehicles would need an enormous amount of capital and expertise to achieve similar results. There are many strategies that can be used to buy and sell property with none of your own money. The formula here will be to acquire $200,000 worth of real estate every two years. At the end of twelve years, a portfolio of $1,200,000 worth of rental property can be obtained. Being conservative and using realistic figures, it is possible to earn $80,000 per year from rental real estate in net (after expenses). Your equity and assets will continue to appreciate through economic times and inflation, making you and your family very wealthy. And it is tax-free to a certain limit. Most J.O.B (just over broke) workers must work about 25 years between 65 and 90 before they retire just to earn that in gross.

CHAPTER 20

Exploring Stock Market Investments

According to experts, being very conservative and putting your money only in savings is not a good idea. Regardless of your financial goal, there is a lot of work that needs to be done along the way, often these goals take years to be achieved, so on the first day the best investment should be made, which offers a better return than savings - even for cases that you say "I will invest my money for less than a year". Remember that a 12-month investment is long term. Because of the current long period of social isolation due to a pandemic, which favors domestic reading than solving doubts that would arise in amounts of 1,000,000 people at the same time, we recommend that you stay at home and search and may even start studying to invest in shares.

Considering the stock market as an investment option is an interesting matter for people who want to diversify their portfolio or have a very long investment horizon. Stock is nothing more than a part of the capital of a company that is divided into several equal parts, which are bought and sold on the stock exchange. Having a stock is the equivalent of having a company. When you buy a share, you become an associated partner of the company and invest your money there, in addition to the possibility of receiving money through what the company profits, at the end of your financial year, are we going to propose that the company distribute part or all of its profit to shareholders in: mention of paying dividends.

CHAPTER 21

Diversifying Your Portfolio

Making a safety net. While on the road to achieving maximum financial freedom, you could face certain situations, even struggling to properly manage your assets. This period is the best time you should create a safety net. You should consider creating a net that can protect your assets for at least eight years and enable you to live on your own means without needing any help. Having backup is important because it can provide a great deal of financial comfort; it reduces stress and gives you the freedom to pursue new opportunities. Other reasons for creating a safety net include: being able to help family members, solving tough financial situations, and providing for yourself when you can no longer do so. You might want to create a safety net by saving enough capital to cover at least 10-15 years of allowance.

Diversifying your portfolio. After you have been active in spending, selling, and investing, you might end up owning assets that were bought for a variety of different prices. This could mean that, because of value fluctuations, some of your properties might lose significant value for certain periods of time. A single stock, for example, may lose half of its value in a matter of years. If all of your savings are invested in it, you can lose half of everything you earned. To avoid such situations, you are advised to invest in a variety of assets that do not follow the same market trends. Using this method, you can achieve the highest level of diversification of your assets by purchasing numerous different stocks from various markets, along with different types of bonds. You could also minimize the chance for risk by purchasing various business sectors, such as real estate and commodities. To avoid market and price volatility, you should buy assets with low or negative correlation. Unfortunately, there might be times when markets continue declining, despite the diversification of your portfolio. During such tough periods, it is important to endure and not exit the market investments. You should stay consistent with your investments and keep buying assets for the long term.

CHAPTER 22

Understanding Risk Management

The objective is not pegged to profits but the determining of both the risk and the maximum amount of risk that the trader is willing to take.

Elegance is: 1. Is a trader interested in open positions? 2. In profits not yet reached? 3. In profits already booked and left in a position? 4. Losses not yet reached? 5. Losses already reached?

Emotional Energies: Money skillfully managed releases creativity and develops internal potential and the ability of self-knowledge. Stress releases substances that will inspire escape strategies that do not find in agreements with objective thought. This is where is the importance of selecting the more suited trader, technical and psychological. The program must follow the twenty-one points that we have already had the opportunity to analyze and possibly re-discuss after each operation. A good strategy is one that decreases tension and consequently stress. Little tension increases frustration, while flexing leaders to make them enter greed long.

The False Solution: For a decennial statistical calculation, investors willing to invest in real estate want an annual return of a minimum of 10%, while trading starts, on average, with a risky profit of 5% per month. High profits, without the intelligent use of work-shop, are synonymous with a future black hole. Why Junior Business respondents manage to generate a capital inflow of ten million earn-ings become internal to the system after 24 months? They are not tame and tenacious, but try and understand strategies not yet di-gested document after document follow-up in addition to mock simulations.

CHAPTER 23

Building a Financial Support Network

It's important for you to understand that financial planning is a highly specialized field. Rules and regulations governing financial planning and products change yearly. Laws and the advisors' products may change over time, and these changes may worsen your financial investments. The following are some common ploys that could have a negative financial effect: - Cold-calling investors. Many aggressive brokers obtain a mailing list and randomly call investors, focusing on those who are at least 55 years old. These tactics have churned up losses for those who were scammed. Guarding against such attacks includes securing an exemption from the National Do Not Call list. - Identity theft. Those who are perpetrating identity theft typically call their victims and ask for personal financial information. Never give personal information over the phone. If you consider the solicitor a legitimate business, ask to mail the information to them. If ID theft suspects do steal personal information, take the appropriate steps to protect yourself. File a complaint with the Federal Trade Commission and alert your local law enforcement. Also, contact the major credit-reporting agencies and provide them a fraud alert. Following these steps may prevent victimization.

Financial Planning Notes of Caution

Nurturing and using a personal and professional financial support network is a required skill in today's fast-paced world. Daily, we need to work with and learn from various specialists, such as appraisers, real estate agents, mortgage brokers, financial advisors, financial planners, estate-planning attorneys, accountants, and other professionals. To grow financially, we need to seek out individuals who have expertise in areas that influence our financial health. We also need to expand our financial network by networking with others who actively work to build financial health throughout their daily lives.

CHAPTER 24

Navigating Economic Changes

Follow the plan:

24 months—Before jumping the gun and investing any savings, you need to do three very important things: - Sit down and figure out your existing expenditures. - Figure out how you can increase your income without using up an exorbitant amount of your time. - Start living on a tight, well-conceived budget. That's what a realistic financial freedom run should be: two years of intense concentration on your finances.

When you finish, you need a place to store and grow your investment until you retire, regardless of your age (no short-term investing!) at which point you need to have access to the cash you've been investing all along. You'll be living off the cash in your investments after retirement. You'll want to set up a diversified long-term buy and hold. LTBH is a strategy used to not have to pay as many income taxes over the years, but it also encompasses the concepts related to dividend health and mid-to-retirement portfolio expansion after plan completion. Makers aren't just boring people who don't know how to have any fun.

24–36 months—Once you're doing right by your money, about two years in with this step-by-step plan, it is time for you to gradually expand the latter part of this time interval. Don't try to cut short the first year of your savings template.

Concurrent with executing the above personal economic changes inherent in living on an established budget, you should prepare for any potential disruptions in your living situation with lessons 4 and 5 of "Poor Couple's Retirement" (used and new) Common Senses or read their equivalent contents in the free version of the Super Blog. Later lessons of "Poor Couple's Retirement" provide a quick review of the first five lessons of the book.

CHAPTER 25

Maximizing Your Earning Potential

The wrong way: Passive person

You may be participating in projects from beginning to end, but this passive person is still actively waiting for wealth to arrive. He or she is convinced there will come a day when compensation deservedly catches up with his or her level of expertise. Note, this does not say "ignorance," which a passive person probably never delivers. It says "expertise." Bright people who go passive (which can take minutes to years depending on the person) typically meld into the culture of their company or situation. Decades go by in the blink of an eye. They are so busy being busy, waiting for the expected financial reward to find its way to them, that they don't take a minute to look at their lives and figure out how to change the one thing they actually have control over.

The right way: Passionate and persistent person

It often comes to mind that true integrity has its lessons built within its approach to remuneration. Those whose honest toil becomes the foundation of our personal wealth can draw huge satisfaction when we plot an ongoing course to work in that manner by ensuring our personal development plan includes obtaining our personal list of skills, saving money to purchase the assets required, and unrelentingly looking to negotiate for bettering our financial situations. Warfare with financial poverty can only be sustained when both these elements are passionately studied and built upon. Then there will be the economy required to purchase the assets needed to initiate an earlier start to our families' personal walks towards financial freedom. Focus when you are there! In battle, the need to concentrate resources is key, however, in our ongoing war against financial poverty our preparation strategy needs to encompass studies that will be the foundation to our new wealth's creation.

CHAPTER 26

Leveraging Technology for Financial Success

Wanting success is one thing, leveraging technology to help you on your path to success is another. If you don't leverage technology to help you get to where you want to be, you will have to work harder and are much more likely to face far more challenges. There is a difference between modern technology and traditional technology. For instance, online web browsing, texting, emails, document sharing, the internet, social media, and more are all modern technology. Writing, sending, and receiving letters; meeting someone face to face; and conducting your researches on foot are traditional technology. Technology is important to our everyday lives as we are immersed in all of it. With technology, we can automate the routine activities, gain insights and experiences, and can streamline our decision-making. No longer do you have to spend an entire day at a dealership to complete a transaction when you can spend maybe 15-30 minutes on the internet.

When you go to a dealership to buy a car, do you just make your decision solely based on some recommendation that you may have heard from a friend, or do you just take the salesperson's word for it? Those are all important, however, there is a lot more to be considered. Everything from the manufacturer, model, dealer's reputation, etc., to the special features that you may want or not. In terms of technology, you should also consider, but not just limited to, topics such as security, cost, ease of use, speed, portability, compatibility, flexibility, upgradeability, applicability, convenience, and customer feedback. Some of these topics we will discuss in the rest of this chapter.

CHAPTER 27

Balancing Work and Life

Your health is most important – you come first. What you eat and drink – if you do not power your physical body daily, if you do not drink enough water and consume too much coffee and hard liquor; if you eat the wrong foods and eat erratically, your health will deteriorate. Every day, keep your body and mind healthy. Please drink ample water, have regular meals, plenty of fruits, and some vegetables. If you find that you catch colds and flu often, you will need to consult a physician to check whether this is the beginning of stress and also find out why the immune system is weak. Stress is capable of weakening the immune system. Of value is to have a routine plan for exercises. Regular exercises are a must. Keep the blood circulation active. Plan a time for walking – remember, fresh air and sunshine are great healers. Keep in contact with family – your top priority. Hug, kiss, and have fun with your children. Take special time off for family, and Duke-of-Edinburgh awards for your child are memorable and deeply challenging team-building exercises. Keep weekends sacred for family at all times. Have family photos on your desk where you work. Family comes first – you need them as much as they need you. Offer help to others with less than you. Reflect and plan how you can help others. Recall your early years when you could truly identify with the poor and needy. Have an internal philosophy of time. After all this laborious work, you may, at best, live to the ripe age of 100. You need time to enjoy with the family, children, grandchildren, and retirement. After the hectic work, retirement would seem a natural time, but also enjoy an interim semi-retirement or spend your time with innovative research. Run a hospital in relation to your age.

Balancing work and life: Work-life balance is easy, work or hard work? Working is hard work, but life has to have some hardness also. I truly believe that no matter how independently we live, we should never give up on our aim of achieving thoughtful and balanced work and life. To be good with all mankind, one has to be good to oneself. Strive towards successful work-life balance. The faculty should make sure that he/she does not have a mundane, boring lifestyle. Each person is unique, but the following suggested balance may be good for general health and peace of mind. First and foremost is to have regular spiritual prayers to keep the mind focused and always approachable and soft. Always foster family contacts frequently. Have healthy meals, good sleep, regular exercise, and have a positive approach to work with persistent hard work. No family member has the right to criticize the faculty for not giving them time, since it is always the quality, not quantity. No one can turn back the clock. Always post your achievements and difficulties on your bedpost to rightfully sleep with peace, as proof of your successes and your efforts to overcome concerns.

CHAPTER 28

Teaching Financial Literacy to Children

To skip any one of these two from the teach financial literacy message would be a disservice to that child. While your financial position alone does not make you happy, good money management can certainly influence the amount of time you get to spend doing the things that make you happy, and that is exactly what most parents want for their children. Not to mention the fact that if they grow up to be financially secure and have a strong grasp of financial literacy themselves, they may be more able to provide for you in your later years.

As with all activities, the most important message your children receive is through your actions. If you are reading this ebook, you are already on the right track. And with every step you take along this pathway towards a future that is always improving, you are reinforcing the most important message of all, regardless of the words that are spoken to explain what you are doing. If you don't implement strategies to improve, no matter what you say, it will be that example that sticks. This is a very important message for your children. It doesn't matter what your starting point is. All that really matters is the direction you are taking and the distance that is travelled.

There are a number of activities you can do with your children in order to start fostering good attitudes toward money, even at quite young ages. Whether they are toddlers or in their teens, they can do these activities. Most, if not all of them, will not only contribute to their development of good attitudes about money, but also many other important life skills. These activities might even help you to start practicing good money management. What a win!

CHAPTER 29

Giving Back and Philanthropy

By adding emergency funds to the individual IRAs and adding annual donations in this strategy, it gives those enough cushion to wipe out any remaining stake. On the other hand, seven percent is not as advantageous as the six percent return, plus a two-year cushion would result in a necessary one-time payment on all cards to average four percent plus the six percenter; in that way, they would still retroactively pay off their cards in lockstep fashion with the tax plan effective tax review.

As an example, a small one-time check combined with annual contributions and non-deductible contributions to a couple through 15 years led to an extra $50,000 cushion if all were comped well. It would be possible to take a tax advantage deduction of $500,000 that enabled an extra $180,000 cushion over the same years. Since these charitable contributions would reduce taxes, giving you an extra $15,076/yr. net donation, it effectively grants an extra $4,500 per year, giving you an aggregate $89,000 cushion. If those funds were left over to be comped, the additional market growth cushioning alone could fund an additional repayment of $32,000 and be an aggregate $242,000 plus cushion once combined with the additional allotted market growth repayment and accounts totaling to an average of six percent from those combined accounts. Keep in mind your tax plan may change some variables. Since the donations might be grandfathered into unlimited transfers of resources or assets into a donor-advised fund (DAF), or a charity, this is like doubling the tax advantage.

At some point, as you pass the retirement milestone, you may want to consider gifting your money or other assets to charity as a tax advantage move. Let us compare your government's use of money and a charity's given you have a certain amount of disposable income. If you pay certain property tax, sales tax, or income tax rates, would you rather pay those monies to your government or provide food, education, medical attention, social services, and recreation to those in need? Once you reach the right level of Net Residual Wealth, donor-advised funds (DAFs) may maximize special lifetime goals. Your DAF can receive recommendations for any DAF asset management firm.

Philanthropy often returns more benefits to the giver of the gift than to the recipient. This is why giving back must become part of your financial plan. It is good to give back to others in need.

CHAPTER 30

Planning for Unexpected Expenses

Emergency Funds

Now that you have paid off your consumer debts, built a positive net worth, and already started a saving behavior, it is time to protect these assets during an emergency. Normally, people use investments as an emergency fund, but it is not advisable practice. The main idea of having an emergency fund is to be like cash, readily available when there is an emergency. We recommend having at least 6 times your monthly average expenses before starting to invest. If you have dependents, then consider a minimum of 12 times your monthly average expenses. But you should feel if 6 months of expenses are good enough to recover from certain events such as a layoff, unexpected health expenses, etc. becomes an emergency. Keep this in an easily accessible savings account. Now you should have been clear what an expense means to you and why you are creating an emergency fund. So let us see how to calculate the money needed.

Let us say your average monthly expenses are Rs.20,000. Then you should have an emergency fund = 6 times * 20,000. If you have dependents, then the emergency fund = 12 times * 20,000. This money will always be considered as an emergency fund and should be replaced and available for meeting expenses in case of unexpected situations. If you will be keeping this money for a longer time, you should make sure to have the money working for you by placing them in a safe investment such as savings deposit as helpful in low interest, other liquid investments. This fund should be used for appropriate purposes only. If you have an emergency and used up the funds in the emergency fund, ask yourself whether it is really an emergency. If it is so, then use a part of this fund and recover it back at the earliest under any emergency fund conditions, then add the possibility of a delay. This way is better. When you don't use an emergency fund, understand the nature of the emergency. Then it is always helpful in protecting your assets. Plan it in such a way that both will happen again through appropriate steps.

CHAPTER 31

Maintaining Financial Freedom

You must create the blueprints of your financial freedom life and keep the space where you plan to achieve your goal absolute. Mark on your calendar the moment you will live financial freedom. Visualize, concentrate, and create a picture of this moment. Assist in managing seminars focused on this subject every year for those who want to continue on the financial freedom path. Continue to pursue the path of financial freedom to maintain the high energy to be a reference for your partner and to ensure that any families that you will help in the future, your children's families, as well as any family members you encourage, will also make this decision positively to walk the financial freedom path.

For financial freedom to be a reality in your life, you must have a clear goal of where you want to reach your path. Many people have the wrong mentality to seek financial freedom, which is to live in the present. They do not plan for the future. The necessary tranquility and security for financial freedom to be fully and completely appreciated, from those who have already achieved it, motives are only to create more wealth and to help others. So write down on a piece of paper all the materials that will help you reach your goal and all the negative emotions that you will need to deal with. Your successful financial freedom will depend on you putting this list into practice every day, changing your routine, and improving your life.

At last, you've hit your goal of succeeding on the path of financial freedom. You've finished the best money adventure on the market. You have driven through the scenery, faced challenges, faced surprises, achieved amazing victories, and you deserve to know how to maintain financial freedom. You now have a guarantee that you will face this new and amazing stage with total safety and no worries. Learn the correct way to raise children who are prepared for financial freedom and teach them everything you have learned. Advise family members to take the financial freedom path. Retake the path of financial freedom and jump into the future to the power of ten.

CHAPTER 32

Conclusion

This world is rich in opportunity, but only for those who strive to become truly wealthy. Recognizably wealthy people always talk about wealth as being initially an inward journey, a journey in which they learn and practice the rules that govern wealth and success. This inward journey is common to people who go from rags to riches. When rags are turned to riches, the habits of the wealthy automatically develop because the poor and the unsuccessful are defined by their one or two personality flaws. In most cases, a decisively applied, positive change brings success. The successful wealthy frugal accumulators have turned inward to find those points of disharmony that knowledge can correct. It is inaccurate to think that the habits of frugal accumulators never change. The lives of these fortunate people trace a circular arc running from knowledge to wealth and back to knowledge. In this never-ending learning loop, wealth becomes a manageable responsibility and the habits become a permanent set of loving tools, tools used to lift others from humble to great beginnings.

"Sow a thought and you reap an action; sow an act and you reap a habit; sow a habit and you reap a character; sow a character and you reap a destiny." We are what we repeatedly do. We create our own destiny. This is why the habits of the wealthy are so important, and why they require constant reinforcement. The seven simple habits and four character-building activities, when practiced persistently, will put you firmly on the road to financial freedom. The richest men and women in the world are virtually all "frugal accumulators" – that is, they save and avoid debt. They also make and maintain advantageous relationships, and they doggedly do what they love for a living.